1/09

PARENT-TEACHER COLLECTION

A Guide for Using

The Cay

in the Classroom

Based on the novel written by Theodore Taylor

This guide written by

Cathy Gilbert, M.S. Ed., and Ph

D1300595

Teacher Created Resources, Inc.
6421 Industry Way
Westminster, CA 92683
www.teachercreated.com

ISBN: 978-1-55734-447-2

©*1992 Teacher Created Resources, Inc.*
Reprinted, 2008

Made in U.S.A.

Edited by
Cathy Gilbert, M.S. Ed.

Illustrated by
Keith Vasconcelles

Cover Art by
Sue Fullam

Table of Contents

Introduction

A good book can touch our lives like a good friend. Within its pages are words and characters that can inspire us to achieve our highest ideals. We can turn to it for companionship, recreation, comfort, and guidance. It can also give us a cherished story to hold in our hearts forever.

In *Literature Units,* great care has been taken to select books that are sure to become good friends.

Teachers using this unit will find the following features to supplement their own valuable ideas.

- Sample Lesson Plans

- Pre-reading Activities

- A Biographical Sketch and Picture of the Author

- A Book Summary

- Vocabulary Lists and Suggested Vocabulary Activities

- Chapters grouped for study, with each section including:
    - *quizzes*
    - *hands-on projects*
    - *cooperative learning activities*
    - *cross-curriculum connections*
    - *extensions into the reader's own life*

- Post-reading Activities

- Book Report Ideas

- Research Ideas

- Culminating Activities

- Three Different Options for Unit Tests

- A Bibliography of Related Reading

- An Answer Key

We are confident that this unit will be a valuable addition to your planning, and we hope your students will increase the circle of friends they have in books.

Sample Lesson Plan

Each of the lessons suggested below takes one or more days to complete.

Lesson 1
- Introduce and complete some or all of the pre-reading activities found on page 5.
- Read "About the Author" with your students. (page 6)
- Read the book summary with your students. (page 7)
- Introduce the vocabulary list for Section 1 (page 8).

Lesson 2
- Read Chapters 1–3. As you read, place the vocabulary words in the context of the story and discuss their meanings.
- Play a vocabulary game. (page 9)
- Build a model raft. (page 11)
- Represent different points of view. (page 12)
- Write editorials. (page 13)
- Begin reading response journals. (page 14)
- Administer Section 1 quiz. (page 10)
- Introduce the vocabulary lists for Section 2 (page 8).

Lesson 3
- Read Chapters 4–7. Place the vocabulary words in context and discuss their meanings.
- Choose a vocabulary activity.
- Write a journal of Phillip's feelings. (page 16)
- Write messages of distress. (page 17)
- Translate Timothy's words. (page 18)
- Experience blindness. (page 19)
- Administer Section 2 quiz. (page 15)
- Introduce the vocabulary list for Section 3 (page 8).

Lesson 4
- Read Chapters 8–10. Place the vocabulary words in context and discuss their meanings.
- Choose a vocabulary activity.
- Role-play experiences in the book. (page 21)
- Discuss trust and friendship. (page 22)
- Draw a map and plot a course. (page 23)
- Write about a personal experience. (page 24)
- Administer Section 3 quiz. (page 20)
- Introduce the vocabulary list for Section 4 (page 8).

Lesson 5
- Read Chapters 11–14. Place the vocabulary words in context and discuss their meanings.
- Do a vocabulary activity. (page 9)
- Create a "jumbi." (page 26)
- Play descriptive matching game. (pages 27–28)
- Research different types of fishing and create a travel brochure. (page 29)
- Administer Section 4 quiz. (page 25)
- Introduce vocabulary list for Section 5 (page 8).

Lesson 6
- Read Chapters 15–19. Place the vocabulary words in context and discuss their meanings.
- Make choices about survival. (page 31)
- Illustrate the storm. (page 32)
- Prepare a plan for emergencies. (page 33)
- Describe and illustrate a survival technique. (page 34)
- Administer Section 5 quiz. (page 30)

Lesson 7
- Discuss any questions your students may have about the story. (page 35)
- Assign the book report and research projects. (pages 36 and 37)
- Begin work on a culminating activity. (pages 38, 39, 40 and 41)

Lesson 8
- Administer one, two, and/or three unit tests. (pages 42, 43 and 44)
- Discuss the test answers, opinions, and responses.
- Discuss the students' enjoyment of the book.
- Provide a list of related reading for your students. (page 45)

Before the Book

Before you begin reading *The Cay* with your students, do some pre-reading activities to stimulate interest and enhance comprehension. Here are some activities that might work well in your class.

1. Predict what the story might be about just by hearing the title.

2. Predict what the story might be about just by looking at the cover illustration.

3. Discuss other books by Theodore Taylor that students may have heard about or read.

4. Answer these questions:

   • Are you interested in:

      — adventure stories?

      — stories with historical settings?

      — stories about courageous children?

      — stories about children who overcome obstacles?

      — stories where a character's creativity sparks your own creativity?

   • Would you ever:

      — be able to accept being blind?

      — trust someone you once considered "beneath" you?

      — learn to live off nature, including the sea?

      — be able to persevere in a seemingly hopeless situation?

5. If you became separated from your parents in an emergency situation, how would you feel? Describe how you would cope with your feelings in order to survive.

6. Have you ever met a person who was extraordinary and who made a difference in your life? Describe this person and relate your experience, telling how he or she changed your life or your ideas.

7. Work in groups, or as a class, to create stories of survival either on an isolated island or alone on an abandoned life raft in the open sea.

About the Author

Theodore Taylor was born on June 23, 1921, in the southern town of Statesville, North Carolina. His father was Edward Riley Taylor, and his mother was Elmora Langhans Taylor.

Mr. Taylor attended Cradock Elementary School in Cradock, a working man's town a few miles from Norfolk, Virginia. The elementary school was part of a larger building which served as the high school as well. While he received straight A's in English and history, problems in math caused him to graduate from high school a year late.

Mr. Taylor's writing career began early, while he was in high school. He was a cub reporter for the Portsmouth, Virginia, *Evening Star* from 1934–1939. He continued there as a sports editor until 1942.

His adult education included attendance at the U.S. Merchant Marine Academy at King's Point, New York, and Columbia University where he studied in the American Theater Wing.

When World War II came in 1942, he joined the merchant marines where he was an able-bodied seaman aboard a gasoline tanker in the Atlantic and Pacific oceans. Later he was promoted to third mate. By the fall of 1944, he was drafted by the U.S. Navy as a cargo officer.

After his university studies in New York, he moved to Laguna Beach, California, in 1955 so he could become active in the film industry. He made several film documentaries which took him all over the world. While on these trips he continued to write articles for *McCall's, Redbook,* and *The Saturday Evening Post.*

Mr. Taylor wrote *The Cay* in 1969 and won 11 literary awards for it. It was featured as the Bell Telephone Special on NBC in 1974. Some awards for his writings include: Commonwealth Club of California Silver Medal; Best Book Award, University of California, Irvine, in 1970 for *The Cay*; *The New York Times* Outstanding Books for the year of 1976 for *Battle in the Arctic Seas;* Jefferson Cup Honor Book Award from the Virginia Library Association in 1987 for *Walking up a Rainbow.* Other books written by Theodore Taylor are *The Maldonado Miracle, The Trouble with Tuck, Tuck Triumphant,* and *The Teetoncey Trilogy.*

He has also written a prequel/sequel to *The Cay* titled *Timothy of the Cay.*

6

The Cay

by Theodore Taylor

(Avon Camelot, 1970)

(Available in Canada, Dell Seal; UK, Doubleday Bantam Dell; Australia, Transworld Publishers)

Phillip Enright is a young boy happily living on an island in the Caribbean. The story takes place on the island of Curaçao, the largest of the Dutch islands off the Venezuelan coast. Phillip and his friends have great times pretending that they are saving their town from pirates of old or from raids by the tall-masted ships coming over the horizon. They like to pretend that these ships are Spanish galleons coming to bombard and pillage their town of Willemstad.

One day their wildest imaginings come true and create a nightmare for the boys and the people of the local islands. In February of 1942, German navy submarines appear. The towns of Saint Nicholas and Aruba are hit by shells. Next the Germans focus on Phillip's town of Willemstad where the large oil refineries are making fuels to help the Allies in the fight against Germany. The people of Willemstad watch as the German U-boats sink tanker after tanker in an attempt to shut down the refineries and stop the oil from being sent to England.

The fighting becomes so intense that Phillip and his mother board a ship to return to the United States while his father stays in Willemstad at his job to help in fuel production. When Phillip's ship is torpedoed and sinks, he finds himself on a small raft with a black dockman named Timothy. Hours later, Phillip awakens and realizes he is blind as a result of a head injury. He must learn to work with Timothy in order to survive with very little food and water.

As the raft floats to a small cay, a new stage of adventure begins. Timothy's ingenuity as a survivor and provider leads Phillip to respect and trust him. Although he is blind, Phillip learns to fish and gather food to survive on the cay. Together they make plans to attract attention if airplanes are out looking for them.

Timothy protects Phillip when the cay is ravaged by a hurricane, but when the storm is over, Timothy is dead. Phillip survives alone until he is finally rescued by American sailors. It has been over four months since the ship he left Willemstad on sank. Phillip is reunited with his parents and eventually returns to live in the Dutch islands. His experiences on the cay with Timothy have changed his outlook on life in many ways.

Vocabulary Lists

On this page are vocabulary lists which correspond to each section of chapters. Vocabulary activity ideas can be found on page 9.

Section 1
(Chapters 1–3)

alabaster	destroyer	distilled	calypso	channel
cleats	mutiny	Nazi	flimsy	hinged
hurricane	pitch	pontoon bridge	oil refinery	parched
pilot boat	stubborn	submarine	schooner	sextant
stern	ballast	U-boat	tanker	torpedo

Section 2
(Chapters 4–7)

anxiously	Denmark	dishearten	doused	clump
gasping	glare	harass	haze	drone
langosta	Panama	plunge	scan	ignore
spicy	steel	tensely	triangle	shudder
biscuit	bucking	clammy	cay	

Section 3
(Chapters 8–10)

bamboo	carnival	catchment	crowing	miserable
driftwood	funnel	hum	patient	rare
murmur	mussels	palm fronds	smoldering	squall
reef	satisfaction	scorpions	vines	weaving
stubborn	supports	urchins	dawn	

Section 4
(Chapters 11–14)

abrupt	bearing	cane	convince	coral
damp	dependent	diameter	echo	faint
foundations	grindstone	harsh	hagged	keg
melon	salvage	shocked	skate	slope
sinkers	stranded	tethered	treacherous	voodoo

Section 5
(Chapters 15-19)

bleat	burrow	frame	fury	groped
described	flayed	inspect	lee	jab
gusted	howl	moray eel	rattle	receded
locate	limp	slithering	swirl	tatters
scallop	screech	consciousness	debris	

Vocabulary Activities Ideas

You can help your students learn and retain the vocabulary in *The Cay* by providing them with interesting vocabulary activities. Here are a few ideas.

☐ Guessing the meaning of words before **checking a dictionary** helps students to remember meanings and gives them confidence in their own independent abilities. As you pronounce the words on the list in your introductory lesson, ask students to tell you the meanings of words they already know. Ask them to use the words in sentences to show understanding of the meanings. Do this activity orally so that students can learn from each other in a cooperative rather than competitive atmosphere.

☐ People of all ages like to **make and solve puzzles.** Ask your students to make their own definitions. Divide the class into groups of two to five students. Have students make two sets of cards the same size and color. On one set of cards have them write the vocabulary words. On the second set of cards have them write the definitions. All cards are mixed together, placed face down on a table, and numbered sequentially. A player picks two cards. If the pair matches the word with its definition, the player keeps the cards and takes another turn. If the cards do not match, they are returned to their places face down on the table, and another player takes a turn. Players must concentrate to remember the locations of words and their definitions. The game continues until all matches have been made. You can ask students to make a set to take home to play concentration with their parents.

☐ Have your students practice their writing skills by creating sentences and paragraphs in which multiple vocabulary words are used correctly. Ask them to share their **compact vocabulary** sentences and paragraphs with the class.

☐ Ask your students to create paragraphs which use the vocabulary words to present **science and geography lessons** that relate to the events mentioned in the story.

☐ Challenge your students to use a specific vocabulary word from the story at least **ten times in one day**. They must keep a record of when, how, and why the word was used.

☐ Play **20 Clues** with the entire class. In this game, one student selects a vocabulary word and gives clues about this word, one by one, until someone in the class can guess the word.

☐ Play **vocabulary charades.** In this game, vocabulary words are acted out.

You probably have many more ideas to add to this list. Try them!

Quiz

1. On the back of this paper, write a one-paragraph summary of the major events in each chapter of this section. Then complete the rest of the questions on this page.

2. In the beginning of the story, why are the residents of Willemstad worried and fearful?

   _____

   _____

3. Why have the Germans come to these islands all the way from Europe? What do they want?

   _____

   _____

4. What is Phillip's father's job at the refinery?

   _____

   _____

5. Why doesn't Phillip's mother particularly like it in Willemstad?

   _____

   _____

6. Where are Phillip and his mother attempting to go to escape the threat of the Germans? Why do they choose to go there instead of somewhere else?

   _____

   _____

7. What happens that prevents Phillip and his mother from reaching their destination?

   _____

   _____

8. Who is Phillip's shipmate at sea? Describe him.

   _____

   _____

9. From what you have read so far about Phillip's mother, how do you think she might feel about Timothy?

   _____

   _____

10. Describe Phillip's feelings toward Timothy when they are on the raft.

   _____

   _____

The Raft

In this section we are introduced to various seagoing vessels found in Phillip's turbulent, war-torn world. There is the infamous U-boat which caused Phillip's immediate problem. There are the schooners which Timothy hoped would rescue them. And there is, of course, the old raft that saves their lives. Rafts are the most basic of all water crafts. In this case the raft is merely a collection of planks laid across some oil drums and lashed down.

For this activity you are to construct your own model raft. You may use the following space to list the items that you will need to create your raft. Your model should be approximately 8"–10" (20 cm–25 cm) in size and should include all items that are necessary for you to survive an indefinite time at sea. For example, Phillip's and Timothy's raft does not have a sail, rudder, compass or any other item which might allow them to continue on to Miami. Your model should include all the items that you think are necessary for survival.

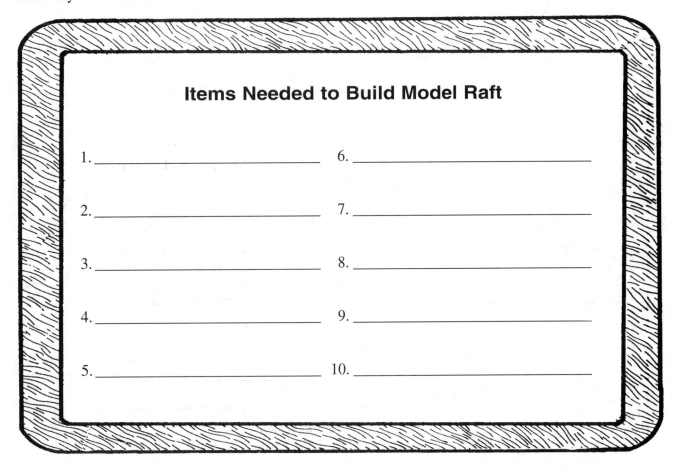

Items Needed to Build Model Raft

1. _____   6. _____

2. _____   7. _____

3. _____   8. _____

4. _____   9. _____

5. _____   10. _____

After you have completed your list, talk with a partner to share ideas and add to both lists to create a better raft. On the back of this paper, make a sketch of your raft to help you visualize the finished product. Remember to keep items on the raft properly scaled to fit. Make provisions to keep necessary items waterproof and lightweight.

You may collect materials for your raft and either bring them to class to work on your project or work on the project at home and turn it in after reading Section 2 (chapters 4–7). Be prepared to share your model with the class. Do you think your model will float?

Points of View

In the first section of *The Cay,* there is not only the global conflict of World War II, but there are a series of conflicts within the Enright family as well. They are being tortured by the decisions which they have to make because of the war. The main question is whether to risk a dangerous trip back to the safety of the United States or to stay on the island.

Phillip loves Willemstad and the island of Curaçao, and he does not want to leave.

Mr. Enright's skills at the oil refinery are needed to speed up production of fuels and to send them to the Allies so they can fight off the German advances. He feels he must remain on the island.

Mrs. Enright longs for the safety of her home in Virginia. She wants protection for her little boy.

Mr. Enright, Mrs. Enright, and Phillip had three different points of view in the discussion about leaving the island.

Write a few sentences for each character, stating in their own words the arguments for leaving the island or staying there.

Mr. Enright   Mrs. Enright   Phillip

Editorials

An editorial section of a newspaper is an appropriate place to express opinions and feelings supported by facts. For the following activity you are to pretend you are a journalist employed by the *Willemstad Winds*, a local newspaper which reports news on this Caribbean island off the coast of Venezuela. Reread the section in chapter two about the Chinese crews on the tankers and how they refused to sail into the dangerous waters without an escort. Write two editorials. In the first one, agree with their decision not to sail without protection and state why it is wrong to bring mutiny charges against them. In the second editorial, criticize the Chinese sailors for not sailing and explain why the people of Willemstad need their help and why the Chinese might be forced to sail or face mutiny charges.

Willemstad Winds   February 12, 1942

Mutiny at Sea

Pro   **Con**

Reading Response Journals

One way to insure that the reading of *The Cay* touches each student in a personal way is to include the use of reading response journals in your plans. In these journals, students can be encouraged to respond to the story in a number of ways.

Ask students to create a journal for *The Cay*. Initially, just have them assemble lined and unlined three-holed paper inside a brad-fastened report cover. As they read the story, they may draw a design on the cover that helps them tell the story.

Tell them that the purpose of the journal is to record their thoughts, ideas, observations, and questions as they read *The Cay*. Provide students with, or ask them to suggest, topics from the story that would stimulate writing. Here are a few examples for the chapters in Section 1.

- Phillip was so disappointed about his parents' decision that he and his mother would return to Virginia that he thought of running away. Have you ever had such disagreements with your family? How did you resolve the problems?

- Phillip was cut off from his family and did not even know whether they were still alive. How would you feel if that happened to you?

- After the reading of each chapter, write one or more new things you learned in the chapter.

- You can choose to draw your responses to certain events or characters in the story, using the blank pages in your journals.

- You may use your journals to record diary-type responses.

- Phillip experiences fear, loneliness, and grief at the beginning of his ordeal. Poets often express strong emotions such as these in their poetry. Try to write a poem that might reflect Phillip's feelings. Remember that poems do not have to rhyme, but they do need to have a rhythm and richness of language to express thoughts that are meaningful to the poet.

- Allow students time to write in their journals daily.

Teacher Note: Evaluation of Journals

Personal reflections should be read by you, but no corrections or letter grades should be assigned. Credit should be given for the effort, and all students who sincerely try will be awarded credit. If a grade is desired for this type of activity, you could grade according to the number of journal entries for the number of assignments. For example, if five journal assignments were made and the student conscientiously completes all five, then he or she should receive an "A."

Non-judgmental responses should be made as you read the journals to let the students know that you are reading and enjoying their journals.

Quiz

1. On the back of this paper, write a one-paragraph summary of the major events in each of the chapters in this section. Then complete the rest of the questions on this page.

2. Where is Timothy from? Why does Phillip think he is from Africa?

   _____

3. In a well-written sentence, describe what suddenly happens to Phillip that makes Timothy feel even more responsible for him.

   _____

   _____

4. Why does Phillip become angry with Timothy and his mother?

   _____

   _____

5. In a few well-written sentences, characterize Phillip in this section. Include his emotions as part of your characterization.

   _____

   _____

6. Why does Timothy tell Phillip to keep away from the edge of the raft?

   _____

   _____

7. How does Timothy attempt to signal an airplane?

   _____

   _____

8. After Timothy sights the cay, what happens to Phillip that enrages Timothy?

   _____

   _____

9. Why does Timothy decide to abandon the raft and go to the desolate island that contains no drinking water?

   _____

   _____

10. In a well-written sentence, tell what you think prevents Timothy from killing the cat?

   _____

   _____

Phillip's Journal

We know that Phillip does not have a pencil or paper on the raft, but if he did, what kind of journal would he keep? Reread chapters four, five, and six to find out the major events of each of the first four days on the raft. Use the space below to make appropriate journal entries, writing from Phillip's point of view. When writing the entries for days two, three, and four, remember that Phillip is blind. He would write about his experiences based on sounds and feelings rather than on things seen.

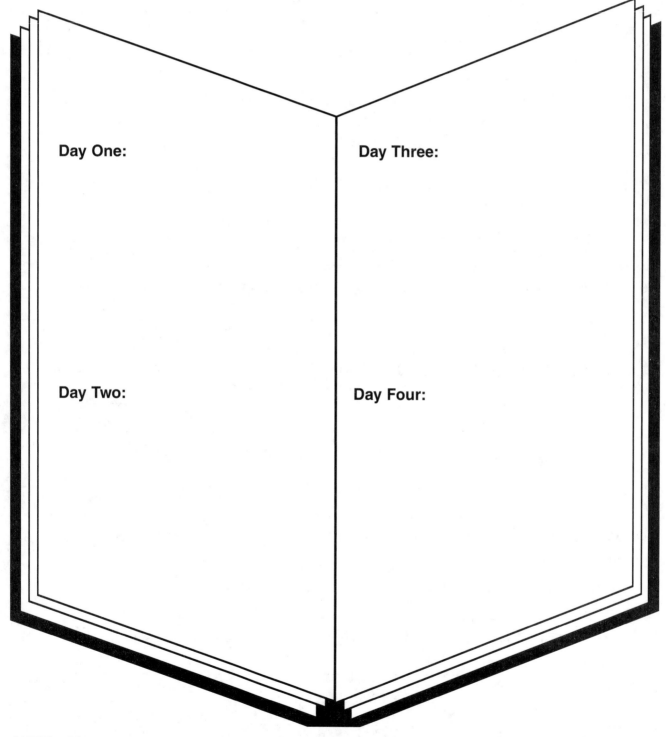

Day One:

Day Three:

Day Two:

Day Four:

Messages of Distress

When Timothy and Phillip land on the cay in Devil's Mouth, Timothy immediately explores the island. He finds that their new home is approximately one mile (1.6 km) long and half a mile (.8 km) wide, and the highest spot is approximately forty feet (12 m) above sea level. The melon-shaped island is one of many in the region. All of the islands are surrounded by a coral reef. Because of the sharp coral, ships avoid the area, and Timothy knows that there probably will not be a ship coming near the island.

Working with a partner, pretend that you are trapped on a deserted island. You and your buddy find an old bottle with a tight-fitting cork. Use the space below to write a message of distress to be launched out to sea in the bottle. Include information that will help the person who finds the message locate you. Describe the island. Give details of where you think the island is on a map.

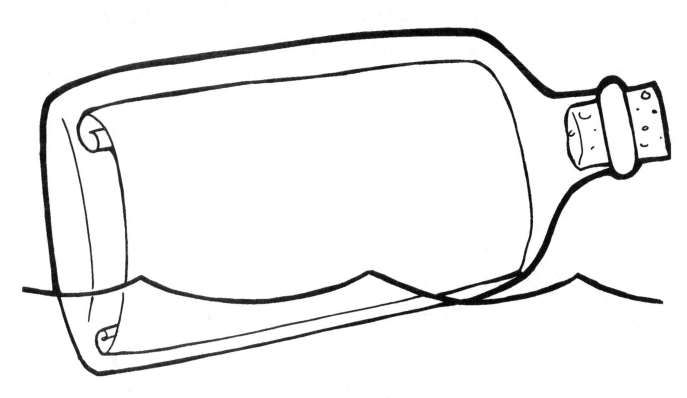

Using the space below, compose a ten-word telegram Phillip might send to possible rescuers. Each word must be carefully chosen to get all the essential information to the receiver of the telegram. Give as many specific details as you can.

TELEGRAM

Translating Timothy's Words

Throughout this and the previous sections we have read Timothy's quite different and colorful English which is sometimes difficult to understand. Do you always know what each word means, or are you sometimes in a hurry and just skip over some of the words? In this activity, you will have time to stop and think about some specific words Timothy uses. Rewrite each of the quotes found below in standard English.

Example 1: Chapter 3   "We 'ave rare good luck, young bahss. D'wattah kag did not bus' when d'raff was launch, an' we 'ave a few biscuit, some cholade, an' d'matches in d'tin is dry. So we 'ave rare good luck."

_____

_____

_____

Example 2: Chapter 3   "Do not be despair, young bahss. Someone will fin' us. Many schooner go by dis way, an' dis also be d'ship track to Jamaica, an' on."

_____

_____

_____

Example 3: Chapter 5   "Dis booby I saw was a blue face, mebbe nestin' out o' Seranilla Bank, mebbe not. Dey be feedin' on d'flyin' feesh. I true watchin' d'birds 'cause dey tell us we veree close to d'shore."

_____

_____

_____

Example 4: Chapter 7   "Young bahss, dere is, in dis part of d' sea, a few lil' cays like dis one, surround on bot' sides by hombug banks. Dey are cut off from d'res' o' d'sea by dese banks."

_____

_____

_____

Example 5: Chapter 7   "D' place I am tinking of is call Debil's Mout'."

_____

_____

_____

Experiencing Blindness

The blow to Phillip's head has severe after effects. Along with the pain, he soon suffers blindness. After he realizes he is blind, he thinks, "I'll never forget that first hour of knowing I was blind. I was so frightened that it was hard for me to breathe. It was as if I'd been put inside something that was all dark and I couldn't get out."

Working in pairs, take turns wearing a blindfold to experience blindness. Choose one of the experiences listed below or make up one of your own. Report to the class after your experience.

Experience 1

Take your partner outside and stop at a variety of places that he or she would recognize well if not blind. See if your partner can identify where he/she is and what is going on. Can he/she recognize voices?

Experience 4

Take your partner to lunch with you. Is eating or drinking juice or water any problem? How about peeling an orange?

Experience 2

Walk aimlessly with your blind friend and at least once "abandon" this friend. Be careful to watch how he/she reacts and make sure there is no safety problem. Return to assist and continue your excursion.

Experience 5

Have your partner participate in one of the class lessons as a blind person. Can he/she keep up with the class? If it requires reading, read for your partner.

Experience 3

Find some type of hazard (stairs, ramp, bike rack, etc.) and carefully guide your partner through this potentially hazardous situation.

Experience 6

Blindfold students while one student stands in the back of the room doing the following activities: crumple a soft drink can, tear a sheet of paper, turn the pages of a book, sharpen a pencil, open a bottle of soda, eat a potato chip. After each action, have students identify the sounds. Have students think of other sounds to perform.

Quiz

1. On the back of this paper, write a one-paragraph summary of the major events in each chapter of this section. Then complete the rest of the questions on this page.

2. Phillip assumes that his father and other men in boats are searching for him, but what does he fail to understand?

   _____

   _____

3. What does Timothy make that he proudly shows to Phillip?

   _____

   _____

4. Phillip is concerned about which two deadly inhabitants that might be on the island?

   _____

   _____

5. Why does Phillip refuse to speak to Timothy when Timothy shows up with three lobsters?

   _____

   _____

6. What does it mean when Timothy tells Phillip, "Young bahss, be an outrageous mahn if you like, but 'ere I'm all you got"?

   _____

   _____

7. What are the two things that Timothy does to help them get rescued from the island?

   _____

   _____

8. Phillip feels good because he discovers that he can do something that Timothy cannot do. What is it?

   _____

   _____

9. What causes Timothy to strike Phillip in the face?

   _____

   _____

10. What does Phillip discover about Timothy that makes him begin to change and to say, "I want to be your friend"?

   _____

   _____

It Could Happen to You

Sometimes it can be difficult to imagine what a character is feeling when experiencing a particular adventure, despite an author's vivid and accurate description. For example, who can really know how it feels to be adrift in the middle of the ocean on a small raft, or how it would feel to suddenly lose the sense of vision, unless one has experienced it firsthand. The experiences outlined below are designed to help the students empathize with certain events in *The Cay*. After each activity, direct students to follow up with a written description of how they felt in that situation.

Confined to a Raft

With masking tape outline a rectangle, approximately 5' x 6' (1.5 x 2 m), on the floor. Pairs of students take turns sitting in the "raft" a specified amount of time.

Direct the students to sit in the raft with no books, no props, no movement out of the space, and no talking to one another. When they write about their experience, they should tell how long it was before they got bored, how it felt to be so confined, and some of the things they thought about while they were "adrift at sea."

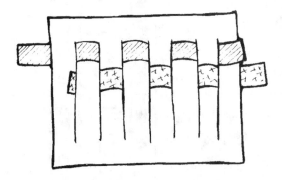

Weaving

Prepare construction paper strips and a pre-cut background for a simple weaving project. Pair the students and let them choose who will be blindfolded first. The sighted partner must explain and help the blindfolded partner to weave a small placemat. Have the partners exchange roles after a certain time. In small groups or in a large group, discuss the difficulties they faced. Was it a frustrating experience for them, and did they feel like giving up right away?

Blind

Ask your parents to assist you with this activity. Choose a day to get totally prepared for school while blindfolded. You must be willing to go to school in the clothes you have chosen while "being blind." Ask your parents to help you go to the kitchen or dining room to eat breakfast while blindfolded. When you get to school, be ready to report on your experiences about what happened and how you felt.

Trust and Friendship

In chapter eight Timothy and Phillip have reached land, and Timothy builds a hut for shelter. As Timothy is working, Phillip reflects on their situation and thinks: "I trusted him that my sight would return in a few days. I also trusted him that an aircraft would spot our fire pile." Neither of these things happen while they are on the cay.

Later in the chapter Phillip is angry with Timothy and thinks: "Sooner or later Timothy would have to understand that he could not ignore me one minute and treat me as a friend the next." Timothy responds to Phillip's anger by saying: "Young bahss, be an outrageous mahn if you like, but 'ere I'm all you got."

Trust, anger, and need are strong forces in friendship. For this exercise, you will meet in groups of four to five people to discuss experiences you have had with your friends. Choose one person to record the key points you discuss. Allow every member of the group to express an opinion in a supportive non-judgmental group situation. Be prepared to present a television talk show style panel to the class to share your discussion ideas.

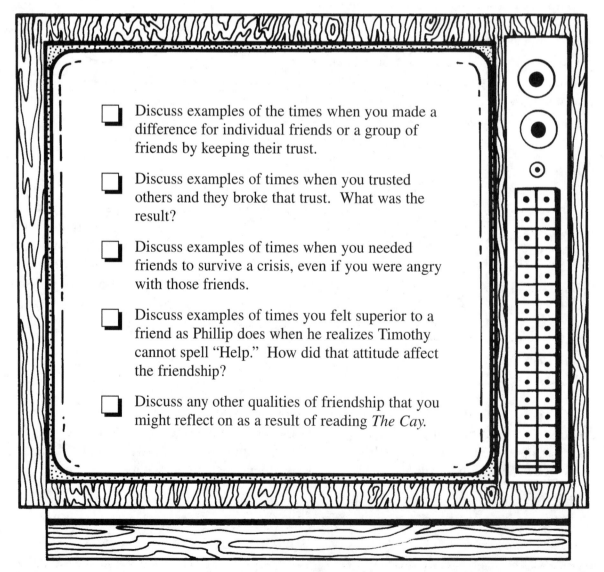

☐ Discuss examples of the times when you made a difference for individual friends or a group of friends by keeping their trust.

☐ Discuss examples of times when you trusted others and they broke that trust. What was the result?

☐ Discuss examples of times when you needed friends to survive a crisis, even if you were angry with those friends.

☐ Discuss examples of times you felt superior to a friend as Phillip does when he realizes Timothy cannot spell "Help." How did that attitude affect the friendship?

☐ Discuss any other qualities of friendship that you might reflect on as a result of reading *The Cay*.

Geography

Sometimes if you can visualize the setting, it helps you to understand a story better. For this activity you are to work with partners, and you will need a geography book, globe, or a world atlas. Turn to the sections on the Americas. Locate the nation of Venezuela. Its map coordinates should be approximately 13° N latitude and 68° W longitude. Panama is approximately 9° N latitude and 80° W longitude.

You and your partner are to draw the geographical region from Venezuela to Miami, Florida, on a large sheet of butcher paper or tagboard. Using the resource books and maps available, outline a map of this area. Label the seas, oceans, and important land masses, including islands. Do not forget Willemstad.

Next, label the latitude and longitude coordinates. Finally, plot Phillip's and Timothy's journey from Willemstad to Panama and on to the Devil's Mouth. Timothy thought that the cay was at 15° N latitude and 80° W longitude. Find that and place a series of small islands there to represent the Devil's Mouth. Use crayons, paints, or markers to complete your map.

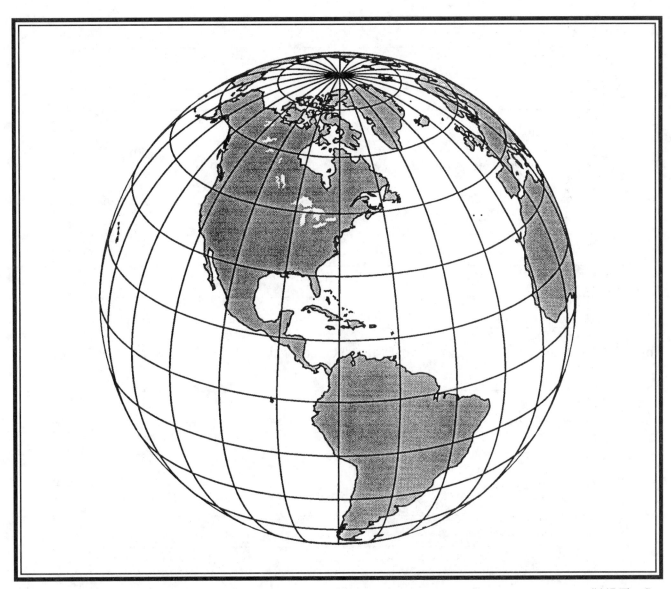

Personal Experience

At the end of chapter nine Phillip realizes "I had begun to change." He says to Timothy, "I want to be your friend." Timothy responds "Young bahss, you 'ave always been my friend." In chapter ten they tell each other about their families and childhood memories. Phillip talks about his parents. Timothy talks about his childhood. Phillip tells Timothy that his mother does not like black people and asks him why. Timothy gives Phillip the only answer that he knows.

Reread chapter ten. Reflect on the changes and increasing maturity that are happening to Phillip as revealed by his thoughts and conversations with Timothy. Choose one of the following topics and write a short, well-organized essay revealing your thoughts on the topic. If you choose to, you may write the essay as a dialogue between yourself and Timothy or yourself and Phillip. If you would rather write a narrative, you may present your ideas in a way similar to the way Phillip reveals his thoughts.

Topic 1: Write about your parents and some of the childhood experiences that you remember.

_____

_____

_____

_____

_____

Topic 2: Write about your views on prejudice and racial attitudes.

_____

_____

_____

_____

Topic 3: Write about an experience in your life which enabled you to say "I have changed."

_____

_____

_____

_____

_____

Quiz

1. On the back of this paper, write a one-paragraph summary of the major events in each chapter of this section. Then complete the rest of the questions on this page.

2. What does Phillip do so that he can walk around the whole island without Timothy's help?

   _____

   _____

3. Why does Phillip think that Timothy is trying to make him independent?

   _____

   _____

4. In a well-written sentence, describe what Timothy says is the cause of all of their troubles.

   _____

   _____

5. What does Timothy finally do to stop the "evil jumbi"?

   _____

   _____

6. What happens to Timothy when he gets that "devil, d'fever"?

   _____

   _____

7. After the fever, what steps does Timothy take to make Phillip even more self-reliant?

   _____

   _____

8. What does Phillip do that convinces Timothy that he is becoming self-reliant?

   _____

   _____

9. What sounds does Timothy hear that indicate that a storm is coming?

   _____

   _____

10. List three precautionary things that Timothy does just before the storm hits the cay.

    _____

    _____

    _____

Chase "d'jumbi"

Timothy believes in voodoo and evil spirits he calls "jumbi." In chapter eleven he uses a Stew Cat jumbi to chase away evil spirits. You may make a jumbi out of wood, a carved bar of soap, cardboard, construction paper, papier mache, clay, craft sticks, computer drawing, three-dimensional painted cat, balloons, or any other idea for materials that you can imagine and work with.

First, list the supplies that you will need. Then plan the steps you must follow to complete your creature. Decide how you can represent chasing the evil spirits away. You may bring the materials to class to work on your project or work on the project at home and present the finished product to the class.

There is no right or wrong representation. Be creative!

Supplies needed:

_____   _____

_____   _____

_____   _____

_____   _____

_____

Steps to complete project:

_____   _____

_____   _____

_____   _____

_____

Plan to chase evil spirits away:

_____   _____

_____   _____

_____   _____

_____   _____

Be ready to share your jumbi with the class on

_____

day/date.

Who? What? Where? When?

In chapter eleven, Phillip gives a blind person's description of the island. Throughout *The Cay,* Theodore Taylor uses descriptive writing to present detailed settings to enable the reader to visualize the scene.

Work with one or two other students to play this matching game of descriptions. The answers are on the game board printed on this page. The descriptions are printed on page 28. Cut out the description cards and place them face down next to the board. Take turns drawing a card and placing it in the correct square on the game board. If you disagree with where a player has put the card, you may challenge the player and present a reason for choosing a different answer. The first team to finish might be the winner if you want to have a class contest.

Henrik (who)	malaria fever (what)	the cay (where)	Stew Cat (what)
the hut (what)	Phillip's mother (who)	before the storm (when)	Timothy (who)
Phillip's father (who)	the palm tree (what)	Virginia (where)	the rain (what)
Phillip (who)	S.S. Hato explodes (when)	the sea before the storm (what)	Chinese sailors (who)

Who? What? Where? When? *(cont.)*

Cut out the cards below to use with the game board on page 27. Match the description to the answer space.

1 It was so still over our cay that we could hear nothing but the rustling of the lizards.	**2** His face was round and he was chubby. His hair was straw colored and his cheeks were always red.	**3** They are very frightened, and some of the people who are angry with them would not sail the little ships either.	**4** Everything was bright red and there were great crackling noises. Heat from the fire washed over us.
5 It was two feet in diameter because I could easily put my hands around to the back...The bark was rough against my hands and feet.	**6** No people. No water. No food. No phones. It was not any better than the raft.	**7** She pulled me up against her body. She was like that. One minute, shaking me; the next holding me.	**8** A crack like d'rifle...It can make d'shot all right.
9 Timothy began to mumble and laugh...He began to shiver again...He never really regained his strength.	**10** I liked it because it was something I could hear and feel; not something I must see.	**11** Something brushed against my arm, and I yelled out in terror.	**12** It was about eight feet wide and six feet deep, with supports made of wood picked off the beach.
13 He didn't just order her to stay. But he wasn't that kind of a man.	**14** He was ugly. His nose was flat and his face was broad; his head was a mass of wiry gray hair.	**15** You are very brown and very lean.	**16** I remembered the summers with lightning bugs and honeysuckle smells; the cold winters when the fields would all be brown.

Fishing/Travel Brochure

The ocean provided Phillip and Timothy with the food they needed to survive. Timothy had great success spearing the fish even though he did not have sophisticated equipment. He taught Phillip to fish with some nails bent into fish hooks, with bolts for sinkers, and with parts of the lifeline for a fishing line.

For this activity, you will be working in small groups to research different ways of fishing. From the list below, choose a type that seems interesting and research it for a report to be presented to the class. Include the rod and reel types that must be used and where you would go to do this type of fishing.

stream fishing	swordfish fishing	tuna fishing
lake fishing	halibut fishing	marlin fishing
deep-sea fishing	trout fishing	lobster fishing
ice fishing	bass fishing	shrimp fishing
pier fishing	mahi mahi fishing	salmon fishing

Create a travel brochure to advertise a holiday for the kind of fishing you have chosen. Include air fare or train fare, hotel accommodations, and car rental in your brochure. Be sure to include prices and information about any fishing licenses as well as special equipment, including clothing that may be needed.

Quiz

1. On the back of this paper, write a one-paragraph summary of the major events that happen in each of the chapters of this section. Then complete the rest of the questions on this page.

2. In a few sentences, describe the storm that hit Timothy and Phillip's island.

   _____

   _____

3. How does Timothy prevent Phillip from becoming seriously injured?

   _____

   _____

4. Why does the storm stop for about thirty minutes?

   _____

   _____

5. What happens to Timothy during the storm and what was the consequence?

   _____

   _____

6. What does Phillip find when he looks for the fishing poles?

   _____

   _____

7. In a well-written sentence, explain why the birds attack Phillip.

   _____

   _____

8. While diving for lobster, what happens to Phillip?

   _____

   _____

9. What does Phillip do to solve the problem of his rescue smoke not being seen?

   _____

   _____

10. In a paragraph on the back of this page, describe the ways that Phillip changes while he is on the cay.

Making Choices

For this activity, you will work in groups of five people. The first task is to choose one person to be the recorder. You will need large chart or poster boards. Using the following list of 15 items, put in order of importance the items you would need most to survive on the cay. Be prepared to defend your reasons for choosing the order of importance. The group must agree by majority vote on the order.

After 30 minutes, each group must choose one member to list their choices, in order on charts. The charts can then be posted around the room. In a class discussion, compare the choices made by each group and decide on any changes you might want to make.

Choice of Items	Priority List
A. Knife	1. _____
B. Matches	2. _____
C. Blankets	3. _____
D. Paper and pencil	4. _____
E. Wood	5. _____
F. Large cloth tarp	6. _____
G. Flare gun and five flares	7. _____
H. Frying pan	8. _____
I. Tin of crackers	9. _____
J. Jug of water	10. _____
K. Hammer and nails	11. _____
L. Rope	12. _____
M. Clothes	13. _____
N. Axe	14. _____
O. Radio	15. _____

Stormy Weather

Working with a partner, reread chapter fifteen. Pay particular attention to words that describe the storm. Take notes, using word clusters to describe the storm. Add more word clusters on the back of this page if you need more room. Use the words to picture in your mind the storm that took Timothy's life and tore the island apart. Then use a separate piece of paper to illustrate the storm, using crayons, markers, or paint. Take your time and produce an art scene you can be proud of.

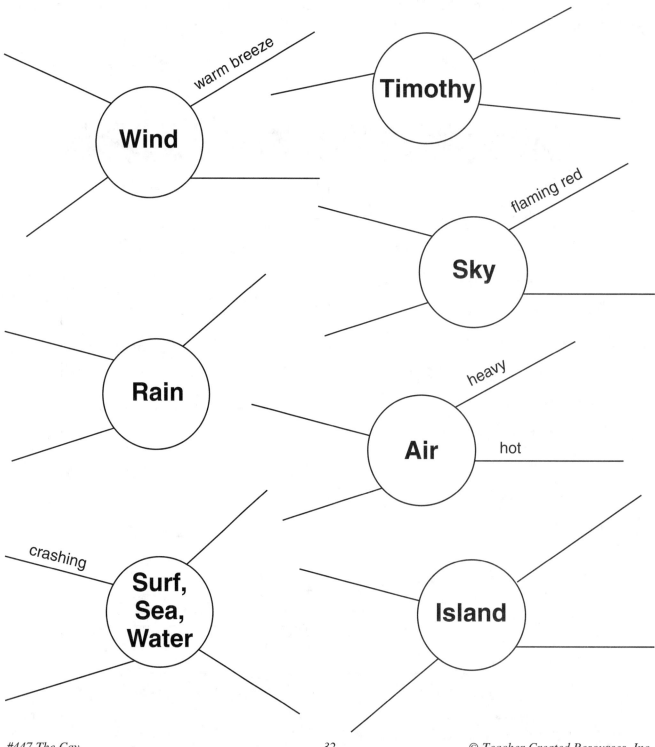

Prepare for an Emergency

When he knows a hurricane is approaching, Timothy prepares the best he can with the resources at hand. He lashes the poles, hooks, and fishing equipment on the lee side of the island to prevent them from blowing away. He lashes the water keg high on the palm trunk and takes everything usable off the raft to a high point on the hill. As Phillip says, "Every day I learned of something new that Timothy had done so we could survive."

As a class, brainstorm a list of natural disasters. When the list is complete, choose one possible disaster and write down the steps you and your family can take to minimize danger and prepare for survival. Be sure to include the supplies you need to gather as well as the actions to take for preparation.

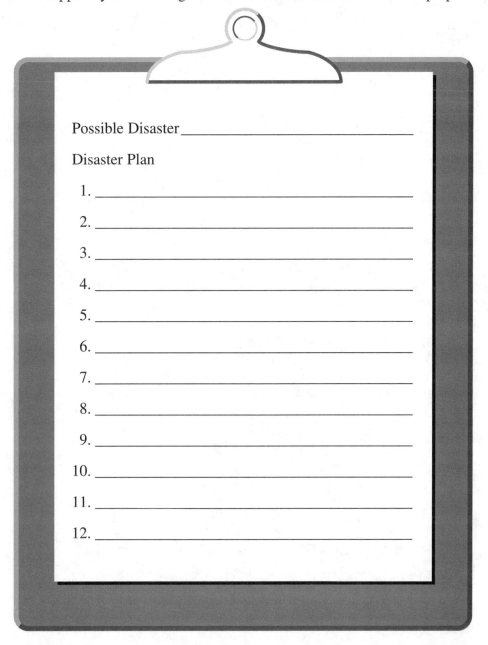

Possible Disaster _____

Disaster Plan

1. _____
2. _____
3. _____
4. _____
5. _____
6. _____
7. _____
8. _____
9. _____
10. _____
11. _____
12. _____

Teacher Note: If time allows, group students by disasters and have them compare their disaster plans.

A Better Way

Timothy did a lot to prepare Phillip for surviving on the island without him. He taught him to fish and encouraged him to climb the coconut tree. He taught him how to light the fire to signal a plane with smoke. Can you think of some techniques that Timothy and Phillip could have used to make their situation even safer or more comfortable? Examples: Could they have devised a plan to turn salt water into drinking water? Could they have created a tool to aid them in retrieving coconuts so Phillip would not have had to climb the tree? Could they have thought of a new way to prepare the fish so it could be saved for days when they could not catch any? Describe something that Timothy and Phillip could have done but did not think of that would have made life on the cay easier. Write about it and draw a picture to illustrate your idea.

Any Questions?

When you finished reading *The Cay,* did you have any questions that were left unanswered? Write some of your questions here.

_____

_____

_____

Work in groups or by yourself to prepare possible answers for some or all of the questions you have asked above and those written below. When you finish, share your ideas with the class.

- Do you think any of this would have happened if the people of Willemstad had had a navy of their own to protect the refinery?

- How do you think Phillip got separated from his mother?

- What do you think Phillip's mother and father did about their missing son?

- How do you think Henrik and his friends reacted when they heard that Phillip was lost at sea?

- Why didn't the Germans just take the refinery with their army instead of surrounding it?

- Did Phillip ever overcome his prejudices because he had spent time with Timothy?

- How would the story have been different if Phillip's mother had not been afraid to fly in an airplane?

- What did Phillip mean when he asked, "Timothy, are you still black?"

- Why did Timothy always call Phillip "young bahss" in the beginning of the book?

- If Timothy had survived, would he have done well in Florida?

- Do you think Phillip might ever do charity work for the blind?

- Why do you think that at the end of the book Phillip's mother had no thoughts of leaving the island?

- Did Phillip's mother ever overcome her prejudices against black people?

- What do you think went through the two sailors' minds when they saw the naked, blind boy and the cat?

- Why did Phillip go after Timothy's knife and not the fishing gear?

- Do you think Henrik still thought of Phillip as his best friend after seeing and playing with him when he returned?

- Do you think Phillip ever returned to the Devil's Mouth?

- If Phillip created a headstone for Timothy, how would the inscription read?

Book Report Ideas

There are numerous ways to report on a book once it has been read. After you have finished reading *The Cay,* choose one method of reporting on it that appeals to you. It may be a way that your teacher suggests, an idea of your own, or one of the ways mentioned below.

• See What I Read

This report is a visual one. A model of a scene from the story can be created; a likeness of one or more of the characters from the story can be drawn or sculpted.

• Time Capsule

This report provides people living at a future time with the reasons *The Cay* is such an outstanding book and gives these future people reasons why they should read it. Make a time capsule design and neatly print or write your reasons inside the capsule. You may wish to "bury" your capsule after you have shared it with your classmates. Perhaps one day someone will find it and read *The Cay* again because of what you wrote.

• Come to Life!

This report is one that lends itself to a group project. A size-appropriate group prepares a scene from the story for dramatization, acts it out, and relates the significance of the scene to the entire book. Costumes and props will add to the dramatization.

• Into the Future

This report predicts what might happen if *The Cay* were to continue. It may take the form of a story in narrative, dramatic, or visual display.

• Guess Who or What?

This report is similar to "Twenty Questions." The report gives a series of clues about a character from the story in a general-to-specific order. After all the clues have been given, the identity of the mystery character must be deduced. If the subject cannot be guessed, the reporter may tell the class. After the character has been guessed, the same reporter presents another twenty clues about an event in the story.

• A Character Comes to Life!

Suppose one of the characters in *The Cay* came to life and walked into your home or classroom. This report gives a view of what this character sees, hears, feels, and experiences in the world in which you live.

• Sales Talk

This report serves as an advertisement to "sell" *The Cay* to one or more specific groups. You decide on the group to target and the sales pitch you will use. Include some kind of graphics in your presentation.

• Coming Attraction!

This movie, *The Cay*, is about to be promoted and brought back to local theaters. You have been chosen to design the promotional poster. Include the title and author of the book, a listing of the main characters and the contemporary actors who will play them, a drawing of a scene from the book, and a one-paragraph synopsis of the story.

• Literary Interview

This report is done in pairs. One student will pretend to be a character in the story and steep himself/herself completely in that character's persona. The other student will play the role of a television or radio interviewer trying to provide the audience with the insights into the character's personality and life that the audience most wants to know. It is the responsibility of the partners to create meaningful questions and appropriate responses.

Research Ideas

Describe three things you read in *The Cay* that you would like to learn more about.

1. _____

2. _____

3. _____

As you read *The Cay,* you encountered geographical locations, historical events, cultural diversity, survival techniques, and a variety of sea animals and plants. To increase your understanding of the characters and events in the story, as well as more fully realize Theodore Taylor's craft as a writer, research to find out more about these people, places, and things.

Work in groups to research one or more of the areas you named above, or one or more of the areas that are mentioned below. Share your findings with the rest of the class in any appropriate form of oral presentation.

Caribbean Area

- geographic region
- resources
- islands
- culture
- languages
- economy
- ethnic groups

World War II

- nations involved
- causes of war
- major battles
- involvement of Caribbean
- involvement of United States
- treaties
- historical impact

Caribbean Plants and Animals

- sharks
- mussels
- sea turtles
- coral
- langosta (lobster)
- sea urchins
- crab• skate
- moray eel

After the Rescue

In chapter 19 of *The Cay*, Phillip is finally rescued by some American sailors. He takes Stew Cat and Timothy's knife and leaves the place he has known as home. He is taken to Panama and is reunited with his parents. Later he has surgery, regains his sight, and returns to Willemstad. Phillip plans to return to the small island and find Timothy's grave.

Imagine how surprised his rescuers were when they found out how the blind boy had survived for so many months. Think about how happy his parents were to be reunited with their son and how impressed his friends were when Phillip told them about his adventure. How do you think Phillip felt when he regained his sight?

Choose something that may have happened after the end of the book and write a short skit. Include several characters and write dialogue for a five-minute skit.

Teacher Note: If time allows, let students choose friends to help them present their skits to the class.

Epilogue

Theodore Taylor has written a prequel/sequel to *The Cay* titled *Timothy of the Cay*. The prequel section of the book gives some background of Timothy's life before he boarded the *S.S. Hato*. The sequel section tells about Phillip's surgery and his plans to return to the cay.

Pretend that you have been given the contract by publishers to write the sequel to *The Cay*. Your story needs to answer many of the questions that readers would have about what happened to Phillip. You may write in detail about one experience, such as his eye surgery or return home, or in general about several adventures that follow.

_____

_____

_____

_____

_____

_____

_____

_____

_____

_____

_____

_____

_____

_____

_____

_____

_____

_____

_____

Teacher Note: Encourage students to share their epilogues with classmates.

Illustrated Time Line

At least one major event takes place in each chapter of *The Cay*. This is the way the author develops the plot.

For this activity, you may work alone or with a partner. Create an illustrated time line showing nine major events in the story. First make a list of the events you will include in your time line. Then in each box draw your illustrations and label the chapters in which the events happened. Cut the boxes out and give them in order on a large piece of construction paper.

1. _____   6. _____

2. _____   7. _____

3. _____   8. _____

4. _____   9. _____

5. _____

Remembering a Friend

Timothy dies protecting Phillip from the storm. He ties Phillip to the palm tree and then ropes himself to the tree behind Phillip. Phillip realizes Timothy is close to death when he cannot stop the bleeding from cuts on Timothy's back. When Timothy dies, Phillip's first thought is "he should have taken me with him..." Later, Phillip cries for a long time, remembering all that Timothy had done for him and fearing the future, "being ...blind and alone on a forgotten cay."

At the end of the book, Phillip vows that some day he will go back and find the cay. Pretend that you are Phillip, several years later, returning to Devil's Mouth on a schooner. In the diary below, write your feelings after finding the little island where Timothy is buried. Then inscribe a headstone to honor Timothy.

Dear Diary,

Unit Test

Matching: Match these quotes with the characters who said them.

> **Mr. Enright**   **Mrs. Enright**   **Phillip**
>
> **Timothy**   **sailor**

_____ 1. *"There is more danger in the trip back...than there is in staying here."*

_____ 2. *"They are not the same as you, Phillip. They are different and they live differently. That's the way it must be."*

_____ 3. *"Young bahss, d' wind 'as shift. You'll be warmer on dis side."*

_____ 4. *"Something happened to me that day on the cay. I'm not quite sure what it was even now, but I had begun to change."*

_____ 5. *"You wouldn't believe what's up there."*

True or False: Write true or false next to each statement below.

_____ 1. Phillip's mother was not prejudiced.

_____ 2. Mr. Enright and his family boarded the ship, *S.S. Hato*.

_____ 3. Phillip, at first, did not like Timothy.

_____ 4. Stew Cat died in the hurricane.

_____ 5. Phillip lived on the island for the rest of his life.

Short Answer: Provide a short answer for each of these questions.

1. Where was the *S.S. Hato* bound?_____

2. Why didn't Mr. Enright go with Phillip and his mother? _____

3. Why did the Germans form an embargo around Curaçao?_____

4. Where did Timothy hide Stew Cat while he was killing the "evil jumbi"? _____

5. After Phillip was listed as officially lost at sea, what did his mother do? _____

Essay: Answer these essay questions on the back of this paper.

1. Compare the Phillip you read about in the beginning of the book with the one who returned home at the end. Include physical and emotional changes in your descriptions.

2. Characterize Timothy by examining specific examples of his actions in the book; use supporting details to verify your choice of adjectives.

Responses

Explain the meanings of each of these quotations from *The Cay*.

Chapter 1: *I guess my mother was homesick for Virginia, where no one talked Dutch and there was no smell of gas or oil, and there weren't as many black people around.*

Chapter 2: *I wondered why he didn't simply order her to stay. But he wasn't that kind of a man.*

Chapter 3: *I was thrown from the top bunk and suddenly found myself on my hands and knees on the deck. We could hear the ship's whistle blowing constantly.*

Chapter 4: *I kept looking at him. It seemed there was a film or haze separating us.*

Chapter 4: *'Now young bahss, you mus' lie down an' rest. What 'as happen will go 'way. Tis all natural temporary.'*

Chapter 5: *'D'cat not good luck.' After a moment he added, 'But to cause d'death of a cat is veree bad luck.'*

Chapter 6: *His voice was thick with anger, but in a moment, after he took several deep breaths, he asked, 'You all right, young bahss?'*

Chapter 7: *D'place I am tinking of is call Debil's Mout'.*

Chapter 8: *During those first few days on the island, the times I spent alone were terrible.*

Chapter 9: *'Young bahss, we need sleepin mats. You can make d'mats.'*

Chapter 10: *I remember smiling in the darkness. He felt neither white nor black.*

Chapter 11: *I was starting to be less dependent on the vine rope, and sometimes it seemed to me that Timothy was trying hard to make me independent of him....I knew why.*

Chapter 12: *When he awakened...he was breathing easily and I knew the fever had broken.*

Chapter 13: *For more than a week, I knew he had been laboring over nails to turn them into fish hooks.*

Chapter 14: *I think it was the fifth afternoon of this week that I blurted out to Timothy, 'I'll climb the palm now.'*

Chapter 15: *I touched his back. It felt warm and sticky.*

Chapter 16: *But now, for the first time, I fully understood why Timothy had so carefully trained me to move around the island and the reef.*

Chapter 17: *Ten pebbles had gone into my time can when I decided to do something Timothy had told me never to do.*

Chapter 18: *There seemed to be no hope of ever leaving the cay, yet I knew I could not always live this way.*

Chapter 19: *'I'll say, 'Dis b'dat outrageous cay, eh, Timothy?'*

Conversations

Work in size-appropriate groups to write and perform the conversations that might have occurred in each of the following situations. Be careful to make the conversations realistic.

- The governor of Curaçao meets with the commander of the German submarine squadron to discuss neutrality. *(2 people)*

- Mr. Enright meets with the owners of the refinery to plan the future of the oil industry during the war. *(3 people)*

- Mrs. Enright discusses with Henrik's mother and two other mothers about how to help in the war efforts. *(4 people)*

- Phillip and a few of his friends make plans to hide Phillip when his ship is set to sail. *(4 people)*

- Mr. Enright and three of his male friends are helping him deal with the fact that his family is going to leave the island. What should he do, go with them? *(4 people)*

- The captain of the *S.S. Hato* answers questions from concerned passengers about the ship's safety if faced with attack from the U-boats. *(4 people)*

- The captain of a German U-boat sights the *S.S. Hato* and its civilian cargo heading out of Panama. He discusses with his commander whether or not to attack the ship. *(2 people)*

- The captain of the *S.S. Hato* and three members of the Willemstad press report the *S.S. Hato* has been sunk with members of the crew and civilian passengers being lost. *(4 people)*

- Mr. Enright and the naval commander from Willemstad get the news from a third party that Phillip is still alive and coming home blind. *(3 people)*

- Phillip and the destroyer's doctor and nurse go over the accounts of Phillip's and Timothy's long days on the cay. *(3 people)*

- The two sailors who discovered Phillip tell their story and answer questions about what they found on the little cay. Include descriptions of Phillip and the physical scene they encountered. *(4 people)*

- The grandparents welcome Phillip and his parents when they finally return to the United States. *(7 people)*

- Henrik and two friends meet Phillip for the first time on Phillip's return to Willemstad. *(4 people)*

- Create your own idea for a conversation among characters in *The Cay*.

Bibliography of Related Reading

Nonfiction

Marine Life

Burton, Albert. *Sharks and Whales.* Grossett, 1989.

Johnson, Sylvia A. *Coral Reefs.* Lerner, 1984.

Radlauer, Ruth and Henry M. Anderson. *Reefs.* Children's, 1983.

Oceanography

Asimov, Isaac. *How Did We Find Out About Life in the Deep Sea?* Walker, 1982.

Blair, Carvel Hall. *Exploring the Sea: Oceanography Today.* Random, 1986.

Lambert, David. *Seas and Oceans.* Silver, 1988.

Sharks

Blumberg, Rhoda. *Sharks.* Watts, 1976.

Bunting, Eve. *The Sea World Book of Sharks.* Harcourt, 1979.

Sattler, Helen R. *Sharks, the Super Fish.* Lathrop, 1986.

World War II

Snyder, Louis L. *World War II.* Watts, 1981.

Stein, R. Conrad. *The Home Front.* Children's, 1986.

Related Fiction

Adler, Carole S. *Always and Forever Friends.* Ticknor, 1988.

Arden, William. *Alfred Hitchcock and the Three Investigators in the Secret of Shark Reef.* Random, 1979.

Bauer, Marion Dane. *On My Honor.* Ticknor, 1986.

Byars, Betsy. *The Pinballs.* Harper, 1977.

Cooper, Susan. *Dawn of Fear.* Harcourt, 1970.

George, Jean Craighead. *Julie of the Wolves.* Harper, 1972.

George, Jean Craighead. *The Talking Earth.* Harper, 1983.

Lane, Carolyn. *Ghost Island.* Houghton, 1985.

Mayne, William. *Drift.* Delacorte, 1986.

Paterson, Kathrine. *Bridge to Terabithia.* Harper, 1977.

Ruckman, Ivy. *Night of the Twisters.* Harper, 1984.

Ruckman, Ivy. *This Is Your Captain Speaking.* Walker, 1987.

Shura, Mary Francis. *The Josie Gambit.* Avon, 1988.

Spinelli, Jerry. *Dump Days.* Little, 1988.

Stolz, Mary. *The Explorer of Barkham Street.* Harper, 1985.

Thiele, Colin. *Shadow Shark.* Harper, 1988.

Thomas, Jane Resh. *Courage at Indian Deep.* Houghton, 1984.

Wyss, J.D. *Swiss Family Robinson.* Penguin, 1986.

Answer Key

Page 10
1. Accept appropriate responses.
2. They are at war with the Germans.
3. The refinery is sending oil to England for the war. The Germans want the oil.
4. Phillip's father is an expert at fuel production.
5. She is worried about her family, and she does not like the oil smell.
6. They are taking a boat to Florida and a train to Virginia. Mrs. Enright's family is in Virginia.
7. Their ship is torpedoed.
8. Timothy is on the raft. He is a very old Negro, ugly, with a flat nose and broad face. He has wiry gray hair and a scar on his face. He is very big.
9. She might not approve since she has a fear of blacks. She always warns Phillip that they are "different."
10. Phillip is afraid of Timothy. He is also angry at him for not giving him enough water and food. He also feels superior to Timothy because Timothy is black.

Page 15
1. Accept appropriate responses.
2. Timothy is an orphan from St. Thomas, Virgin Islands. Phillip thinks he is from Africa because he looks like men he has seen in jungle pictures.
3. The problem is that now Phillip is blind.
4. He blames them for his situation.
5. Phillip could be characterized as self-centered.
6. Timothy is afraid Phillip will fall into the shark infested waters.
7. He attempts to generate a smoke flare from a piece of burning cloth on a stick.

8. Phillip falls into the shark infested waters.
9. Timothy decides to abandon the raft so he can signal for help. He also thinks it will be safer away from the sharks.
10. Timothy is afraid to kill the cat because he is superstitious and thinks it would cause bad luck.

Page 16
Day One: He wakes up and finds himself on a raft with a black man named Timothy. Phillip is not blind yet.

Day Two: Phillip discovers he is blind.

Day Three: Phillip hears an airplane. Timothy tries to signal it.

Day Four: Phillip falls overboard, and Timothy saves him from sharks.

Page 18
1. "We have rare good luck, young boss. The water keg did not bust when the raft was launched, and we have a few biscuits, some chocolate and the matches in the tin are dry. So we have rare good luck."
2. "Do not despair, young boss. Someone will find us. Many schooners go by this way, and this is also the ship track to Jamaica, and on."
3. "This booby I saw was a blue face, maybe nesting out of Seranilla Bank, maybe not. They are feeding on the flying fish. I am watching the birds because they tell us we are very close to the shore."
4. "Young boss, there is, in this part of the sea, a few little cays like this one, surrounded on both sides by hombug banks. They are cut off from the rest of the sea by these banks."
5. "The place I am thinking of is called Devil's Mount."

Answer Key *(cont.)*

Page 20

1. Accept appropriate responses.
2. He fails to take into consideration that the war is more important, and everyone is busy.
3. He makes a hut.
4. He is worried about scorpions and snakes.
5. He is angry about being left alone.
6. Timothy is telling Phillip that they better work together and be friends since there is no one else to help them.
7. Timothy prepares an ongoing rescue fire and spells out the word "Help" with rocks and sticks in the sand.
8. Phillip can spell, and Timothy cannot.
9. He strikes Phillip because Phillip refuses to even try to help make sleeping mats. Phillip makes fun of Timothy because he cannot spell.
10. Phillip discovers that Timothy has been making a rope for his safety. Phillip realizes that all along Timothy has been trying to help him.

Page 25

1. Accept appropriate responses.
2. Phillip is able to walk around the island by keeping his feet in the damp sand near the water's edge.
3. He realizes that Timothy is worried that he might die and Phillip will be left defenseless.
4. Timothy says Stew Cat is the cause of their troubles.
5. Timothy solves the problem by putting Stew Cat on the raft. Then he makes a carving of the cat and kills the jumbi by nailing the carving on the roof. The nails drive out the jumbi.
6. The fever drives Timothy into the water. He needs to clear the burning fever from his head.

7. After the fever, Timothy helps Phillip by making extra fishing poles and fish hooks. He takes Phillip to a safe fishing hole where Phillip is able to fish for himself. He teaches Phillip how to use mussels for bait.
8. Phillip climbs the palm tree to get coconuts.
9. Timothy hears the waves crack like rifle shots on the reefs.
10. He lashes the water keg high on the palm tree. He ties extra rope onto the tree for hand and arm holds. He dismantles the raft and saves the parts. He prepares a huge meal in case they cannot eat for days. He gives Phillip cups of coconut milk for nourishment. He lashes his knife to a tree for recovery later.

Pages 27–28

1. before the storm
2. Henrik
3. Chinese sailors
4. *S.S. Hato* explodes
5. the palm tree
6. the cay
7. Phillip's mother
8. the sea before the storm
9. malaria fever
10. the rain
11. Stew Cat
12. the hut
13. Phillip's father
14. Timothy
15. Phillip
16. Virginia

Answer Key (cont.)

Page 30

1. Accept appropriate responses.
2. The storm that hit the island began slowly with dark clouds and a hot wind. Soon the wind was howling, and the rain was pelting down.
3. Timothy put his body between the storm and Phillip to take the brunt of the storm.
4. The storm stops because they are in the eye of the hurricane.
5. Timothy's body is lashed and torn by the storm winds and sand. The result is that he dies.
6. Phillip finds that Timothy has lashed at least twelve poles and many hooks and sinkers to the palm tree for him.
7. The birds attack Phillip because he is in their nesting ground.
8. Phillip is attacked by a moray eel.
9. Phillip gets the smoke to blacken by using the oily sea grapes in the fire.
10. Phillip seems to change by becoming more mature. He becomes self-reliant and stops being prejudiced. He learns to trust someone.

Page 32

Accept all appropriate descriptive words that might fit the clusters.

Page 42

Matching

1. Mr. Enright
2. Mrs. Enright
3. Timothy
4. Phillip
5. sailor

True or False

1. False
2. False
3. True
4. False
5. False

Short Answer

1. The *S.S. Hato* was bound for Panama and then to Miami, Florida.
2. Mr. Enright felt the oil production was necessary to win the war.
3. They were making sure none of the oil or fuel resources reached their enemies.
4. He placed Stew Cat on the raft out at sea.
5. Phillip's mother returned to be with her husband at Willemstad.

Essay

Accept all reasonable and appropriate responses. They should mention that he was no longer as self-centered as he used to be, and he had a greater understanding and acceptance of black people.

Accept reasonable responses and make sure there is evidence to support descriptions.

Page 43

Accept all reasonable answers.